# GEORGIA
# JOURNEYS
## COMMON CORE

Houghton
Mifflin
Harcourt

**Program Authors**

James F. Baumann · David J. Chard · Jamal Cooks
J. David Cooper · Russell Gersten · Marjorie Lipson
Lesley Mandel Morrow · John J. Pikulski · Héctor H. Rivera
Mabel Rivera · Shane Templeton · Sheila W. Valencia
Catherine Valentino · MaryEllen Vogt

**Consulting Author**

Irene Fountas

# Unit 1

Lesson

**3** TOPIC: **School**

# Welcome, Reader!

This year you will read many wonderful stories. In this first book, you will meet lots of pals, a special grandpa, and a curious monkey who gets into trouble. You will read about neighborhood helpers and a cat who takes a ride on a train. Your reading will get stronger each day!

Are you ready to begin your reading journey? Just turn the page!

Sincerely,

*The Authors*

unit 1

What Is a Pal?
by Nina Crews

Friends Forever

☑ **WORDS TO KNOW**
High-Frequency Words

play

be

and

help

with

you

**Vocabulary Reader**

**Context Cards**

**COMMON CORE** **ELACC1RF3g** recognize and read irregularly spelled words

Go Digital

# Words to Know

Read Together

▶ Read each Context Card.

▶ Make up a sentence that uses a blue word.

**1** **play**

These pals like to play in the park.

**2** **be**

They like to be on the same team.

## 3 and

The children share the paper **and** paint.

## 4 help

These pals **help** each other wash the dog.

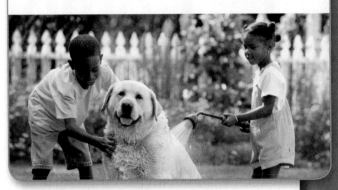

## 5 with

The boy was in a show **with** his pals.

## 6 you

I like when **you** play this game with me.

# Read and Comprehend

☑ **TARGET SKILL**

**Main Idea** As you read, look for one big idea that the selection is about. This is the **topic**. The **main idea** is the most important idea about the topic. **Details** are bits of information that tell more about the main idea. You can list the main idea and details about a topic on a web like this.

☑ **TARGET STRATEGY**

**Summarize** Stop to tell important ideas as you read.

## Friendship

How do pals act?

Pals play together.

They help each other.

Pals take turns.

They are kind.

Pals have fun.

What do you do with your pals?

You will learn all about pals in

**What Is a Pal?**

# ANCHOR TEXT

## ✓ TARGET SKILL

**Main Idea** Tell the important idea about the topic.

## ✓ GENRE

**Informational text** tells about things that are real. Look for:

▶ words that tell information

▶ photographs that show details about the real world

**ELACC1RI2** identify the main topic and retell key details; **ELACC1RI10** read informational texts

**Meet the Author and Photographer**

## Nina Crews

Nina Crews comes from a very creative family. Her parents, Donald Crews and Ann Jonas, are both well-known artists. For her own artwork, Ms. Crews likes to make collages out of photos.

# What Is a Pal?

written and photographed by Nina Crews

**ESSENTIAL QUESTION**

What is important about being a friend?

A pal can help you.

Sam and Nat can help Dan.

A pal can play with you.

Tad, Cam, ⬛ can ben play.

A pal e a pet.

A pal can be Dad.

A pal can be with you.

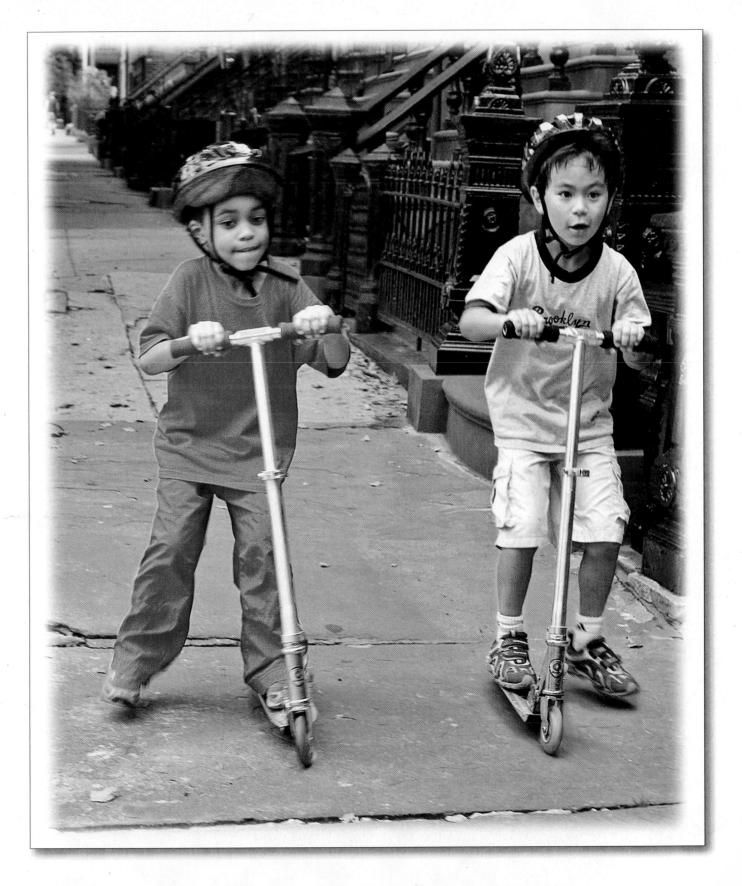

A pal is fun to be with!

Are you a pal?

# Dig Deeper

Read Together

## How to Analyze the Text

Use these pages to learn about Main Idea and Informational Text. Then read **What Is a Pal?** again.

## Main Idea

In **What Is a Pal?**, you read about what it means to be a pal. This is the **topic**. The **main idea** is the most important idea about the topic. What is the main idea? **Details** are bits of information about the main idea. What details did you find out about pals? Use a web to show the main idea and details.

ELACC1RI2 identify the main topic and retell key details; ELACC1RI10 read informational texts

COMMON CORE

Go Digital

## Genre: Informational Text

**What Is a Pal?** has details that are **facts**. Facts are true information. What facts do you learn from the words?

The pictures show real kids who are pals. What information do you learn from the pictures?

# Your Turn

## RETURN TO THE ESSENTIAL QUESTION

Turn and Talk

**What is important about being a friend?** What details does the selection tell about being a pal? What else do you know about being a pal? Tell your partner. Speak in complete sentences.

 **Classroom Conversation**

Talk about these questions with your class.

1 Who could be a pal?

2 What things from **What Is a Pal?** have you done with friends?

3 What words tell about being a good pal?

**Response** Read the last page of the selection again. Write a sentence to answer the question. Draw a picture to go with your answer.

### Writing Tip

Read your answer. Add details to give information. Begin your sentence with a capital letter.

**COMMON CORE** **ELACC1RI2** identify the main topic and retell key details; **ELACC1W5** focus on a topic, respond to questions/suggestions from peers, and add details to strengthen writing; **ELACC1SL6** produce complete sentences when appropriate to task and situation

# POETRY

Friends Forever

**Read Together**

## ✓ GENRE

**Poetry** uses words in interesting ways to show pictures and feelings.

## ✓ TEXT FOCUS

When words **rhyme,** they end with the same sound, like <u>blue</u> and <u>two</u>. Clap when you hear words that rhyme at the end of the lines.

COMMON CORE

**ELACC1RL10** read prose and poetry;
**ELACC1L6** use words/phrases learned through conversations, reading, and response
to reading

Go Digital

# Friends Forever

How can you be a good friend?
You can play with your friends.
You can share with friends and
help them.

## Damon & Blue

Damon & Blue
Just us two
Cruising up the avenue.

You strut, you glide
But mark our stride
Can't beat us when we're
side by side.

*by Nikki Grimes*

# Wait for Me

Wait for me
and I'll be there
and we'll walk home together,
if it's raining
puddle pails
or if it's sunny weather.

Wait for me
and I'll be there
and we'll walk home together.
You wear red
and I'll wear blue,
and we'll be friends forever.

*by Sarah Wilson*

# Jambo

Jambo Jambo
ambo ambo
mbo mbo
bo bo bo
o o o
bo bo bo
mbo mbo
ambo ambo
Jambo Jambo
HI! HELLO!
Did you Did you
did you know
Jambo means
hello hello!

*by Sundaira
Morninghouse*

**Respond to Poetry**

- Listen to the poems again. Join in!
- Say more rhyming lines that could be added to one of the poems.

32

# Compare Texts

**Read Together**

## TEXT TO TEXT

**Compare Friends** How are the friends in the poems like the pals in the selection? How are they different? Make a chart.

| Alike | Different |
|-------|-----------|
| play help | walk in the rain |

## TEXT TO SELF

**Write Sentences** Write sentences to tell your classmates about favorite things you do with your pals.

## TEXT TO WORLD

**Describing Words** Read the poems again. Find words that tell what the friends look like. Find words that tell what they see in their world and help show how they feel.

**COMMON CORE** **ELACC1RL4** identify words and phrases that suggest feelings or appeal to senses; **ELACC1RI9** identify similarities in and differences between texts on the same topic

# Grammar

 Read Together

 Go Digital

**Nouns** Some words name people or animals. Some words name places or things. Words that name people, animals, places, or things are called **nouns**.

## Nouns for People

boy

dad

## Nouns for Animals

dog

cat

## Nouns for Places

house

sky

garden

## Nouns for Things

book

door

bed

**Try This!**

Talk about each picture with a partner. Name the nouns you see. Then write a noun from the box to name each picture. Use another sheet of paper.

| mom | room | city | bird | clock | girl |
|-----|------|------|------|-------|------|

1.

2.

3.

4.

5.

6.

 **Grammar in Writing**

Share your writing with a partner.
Talk about the nouns you used.

# Narrative Writing

✅**Ideas** Dan drew and wrote about his pals and what they do.  Then he thought about what details to add.  He added a picture of a ball and a **label**.

**Revised Draft**

my pal Max

soccer ball

## Writing Traits Checklist

✅**Ideas** Does my writing have interesting details about my pals?

☑ Did I use nouns in my labels?

☑ Did I write letters neatly and correctly?

What do the details in Dan's writing tell you about his pals and what they do? Now revise your writing. Use the Checklist.

Final Copy

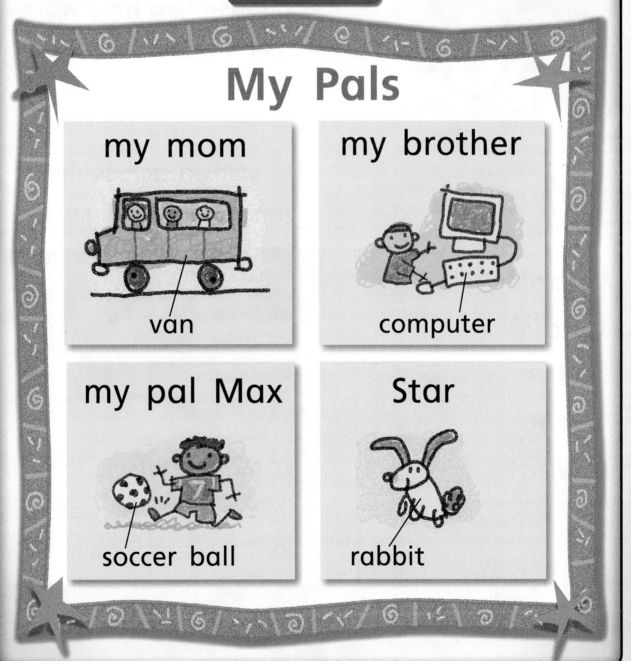

# My Pals

| my mom | my brother |
|---|---|
| van | computer |

| my pal Max | Star |
|---|---|
| soccer ball | rabbit |

# Lesson 2

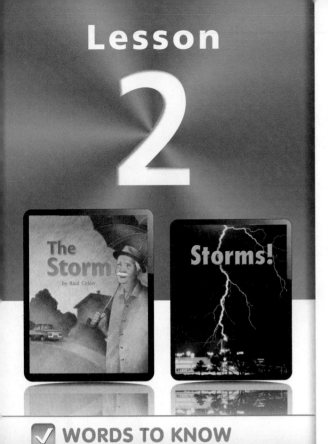

✓ **WORDS TO KNOW**
High-Frequency Words

he

look

have

for

too

what

**Vocabulary Reader**

**Context Cards**

**ELACC1RF3g** recognize and read irregularly spelled words

Go Digital

# Words to Know

Read Together

▶ Read each Context Card.

▶ Choose two blue words. Use them in sentences.

**1** **he**

He walked across the street with his friends.

**2** **look**

Children look at water from the fire hose.

**3** **have**

We have fun seeing the fast fire truck.

**4** **for**

The doctor had a kind smile for Ann.

**5** **too**

They took hats and the sunblock, too.

**6** **what**

What do people do to help you feel safe?

# Read and Comprehend

Read Together

Go Digital

✅ **TARGET SKILL**

**Understanding Characters** The people and animals in a story are the **characters**. Think about who the characters are and what they do. Use story clues, called **text evidence**, to figure out how characters feel and why they act as they do. You can write text evidence in a chart like this.

| Characters | Actions |
|------------|---------|
|            |         |

✅ **TARGET STRATEGY**

**Infer/Predict** Use text evidence to figure out more about the story and to think of what might happen next.

COMMON CORE

**ELACC1RL3** describe characters, settings, and major events; **ELACC1RL7** use illustrations and details to describe characters, setting, or events

40

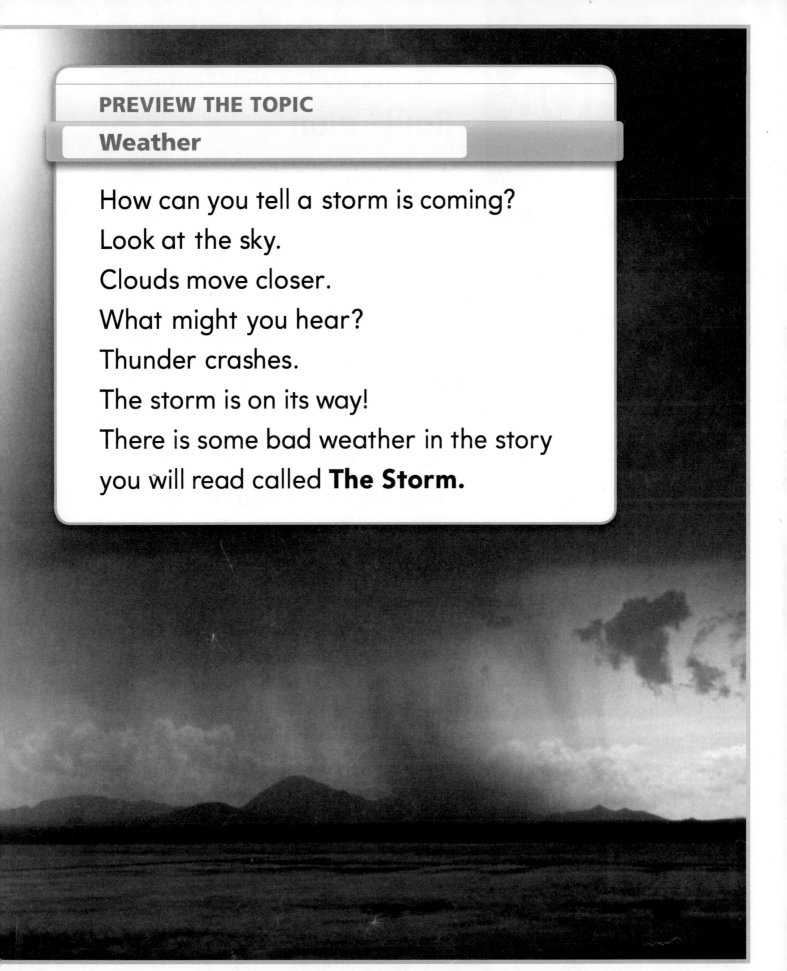

## Weather

How can you tell a storm is coming?

Look at the sky.

Clouds move closer.

What might you hear?

Thunder crashes.

The storm is on its way!

There is some bad weather in the story you will read called **The Storm.**

# Lesson 2

## ANCHOR TEXT

The Storm
by Raúl Colón

☑ **TARGET SKILL**

**Understanding Characters** Tell about characters' actions.

☑ **GENRE**

**Realistic fiction** is a made-up story that could happen in real life. Look for:

▸ things that could really happen
▸ people who act like people in real life

**ELACC1RL3** describe characters, settings, and major events; **ELACC1RL7** use illustrations and details to describe characters, setting, or events; **ELACC1RL10** read prose and poetry

Go Digital

**Meet the Author and Illustrator**

# Raúl Colón

As a little boy in Puerto Rico, Raúl Colón was often very sick. He spent a lot of time inside, drawing. He even made his own comic books. Today, Mr. Colón lives in New York and works as an artist and a writer.

# The Storm

written and illustrated
by Raúl Colón

**ESSENTIAL QUESTION**

What happens during
a storm?

Pop has come in.
Look! He is wet.

Tim and Rip ran to him.

Tim, Rip, and Pop have fun.

Tim had to go to bed.

What did Tim and Rip see?

Tim hid in his bed!
Rip hid, too!

Look what Pop had for Tim.
Tim had a sip.

Pop had a hug for Tim.
He had a hug for Rip, too.

Pop sat with Tim and Rip.

# Dig Deeper

Read Together

## How to Analyze the Text

Use these pages to learn more about Understanding Characters and Realistic Fiction. Then read **The Storm** again.

## Understanding Characters

In **The Storm**, you read about different **characters.** What important things do the characters do? What does this text evidence tell you about what they are like? Use a chart to list the characters and their actions to help you understand them better.

| Characters | Actions |
|---|---|
|  |  |

COMMON CORE

**ELACC1RL3** describe characters, settings, and major events; **ELACC1RL7** use illustrations and details to describe characters, setting, or events

54

Go Digital

## Genre: Realistic Fiction

**The Storm** is a story with a beginning, middle, and end. It is a made-up story, but it could happen in real life.

In **realistic fiction**, characters act like real people. The events could really happen. Think about what happens in **The Storm.** Could it happen to you?

# Your Turn

## RETURN TO THE ESSENTIAL QUESTION

 **Turn and Talk**

**What happens during a storm?** Talk about what happens during different parts in **The Storm** and how it makes Tim feel. Use words and actions to act out his feelings in a group.

 **Classroom Conversation**

Talk about these questions with your class.

1. How does Tim show his feelings?

2. How does Pop help Tim?

3. What does Tim see and hear during the storm?

## WRITE ABOUT READING

**Response** Look at pages 48–49. Write words to tell how Tim feels. Look for text evidence. Use the pictures and the words on the pages to help you.

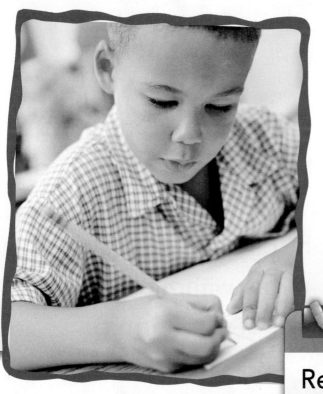

### Writing Tip

Read your answer. Add words that give information.

**ELACC1RL4** identify words and phrases that suggest feelings or appeal to senses; **ELACC1RL7** use illustrations and details to describe characters, setting, or events; **ELACC1L5d** distinguish shades of meaning among verbs and adjectives

Read Together

Storms!

**Informational text** gives facts on a topic. It can be from a textbook, article, or website. Look for storm facts as you read.

**Photographs** show pictures of real things with important details. Use these photographs to find out information about storms.

COMMON CORE

**ELACC1RI6** distinguish between information provided by pictures and words;
**ELACC1RI10** read informational texts

Go Digital

# Storms!

A storm is a strong wind with rain or snow. It may have hail or sleet. Warm, light air goes up quickly. It mixes with high, cold air. Look! It's a storm.

This is a lightning storm in Pampa, Texas.

## Kinds of Storms

A thunderstorm has thunder and lightning. It can bring heavy rain.

A tornado is a strong, twisting wind. It is shaped like a cone.

A hurricane is a very big storm. It has strong, spinning winds and rain.

A dust storm is a strong wind that carries dust for miles.

rain gauge

thermometer

wind gauge

wind sock

## Measuring Storms

Scientists have tools for measuring storms. They measure heat and cold. They measure the wind. They measure rainfall and snowfall, too.

What storms have you seen?

# Compare Texts

Read
Together

## TEXT TO TEXT

**Compare Storms** Look again at the selection **Storms!** Talk about each kind of storm. Which kind of storm did Tim and Rip see? Speak one at a time, and listen to everyone's ideas.

## TEXT TO SELF

**Write Sentences** Write about a time you saw a storm. How did the weather change?

## TEXT TO WORLD

**Connect to Social Studies** How can neighbors help each other in a storm? Draw a picture. Tell a partner about it.

Go
Digital

COMMON CORE

**ELACC1RI9** identify similarities and differences between texts on the same topic; **ELACC1W8** recall information from experiences or gather information from sources to answer a question; **ELACC1SL1a** follow rules for discussions; **ELACC1SL5** add drawings or visual displays to descriptions to clarify ideas, thoughts, and feelings

**ELACC1L1b** use common, proper, and possessive nouns

# Grammar

**Possessive Nouns** Some nouns show that one person or one animal owns or has something. These nouns are called **possessive nouns.** They end in **'s.**

## Possessive Nouns for One Person

a man's hat

one boy's bed

## Possessive Nouns for One Animal

a dog's ball

one cat's tail

**Try This!**

Talk about each picture with a partner. Tell who has or owns something. Then write a possessive noun from the box to go with each picture. Use another sheet of paper.

| man's | bird's | boy's | dog's | girl's | cat's |

1.

a _____ bike

2.

a _____ ball

3.

a _____ book

4.

a _____ food

5.

one _____ hat

6.

one _____ nest

 **Grammar in Writing**

Share your writing with a partner. Say a sentence with each possessive noun you used.

**COMMON CORE** ELACC1W3 write narratives; **ELACC1W5** focus on a topic, respond to questions/suggestions from peers, and add details to strengthen writing; **ELACC1L1b** use common, proper, and possessive nouns

# Narrative Writing

☑ **Ideas** What did Kit's family do at the beach? Kit drew and wrote about her trip. Then she thought of new details. She added a **caption** to explain her picture.

**Revised Draft**

We saw a fish.

 **Writing Traits Checklist**

☑ **Ideas** Does my writing have interesting details about my family trip?

☑ Do my captions explain the pictures?

☑ Did I use nouns to name places or things?

Look for nouns in Kit's final copy.
Then revise your own writing.
Use the Checklist.

**Final Copy**

# Our Trip to the Beach

my family

a castle we made

We saw a fish.

We found shells.

## ✓ WORDS TO KNOW
High-Frequency Words

sing

do

they

find

funny

no

Vocabulary
Reader

Context
Cards

**ELACC1RF3g** recognize and read irregularly
spelled words

# Words
to Know

▶ Read each Context Card.

▶ Ask a question that uses
one of the blue words.

1 **sing**

These children sing
with the music teacher.

2 **do**

The school principal
has many things to do.

### 3 they

They like to work together in class.

### 4 find

The librarian helps children find books.

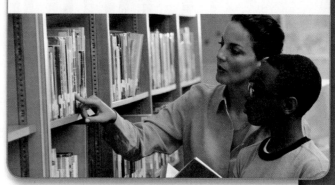

### 5 funny

The art teacher drew a funny animal.

### 6 no

No, you cannot cross until the cars are gone.

# Read and Comprehend

Read Together

Go Digital

## ✓ TARGET SKILL

**Sequence of Events** Many stories tell about events in the order in which they happen. This order is called the **sequence of events.** The sequence of events is what happens **first, next,** and **last** in a story. You can use a flow chart like this to write about the events in a story.

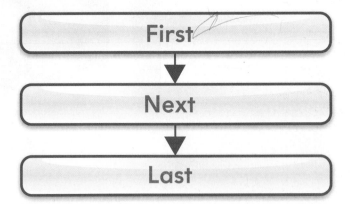

First

↓

Next

↓

Last

## ✓ TARGET STRATEGY

**Monitor/Clarify** If part of a story doesn't make sense, read that part again.

**ELACC1RL3** describe characters, settings, and major events

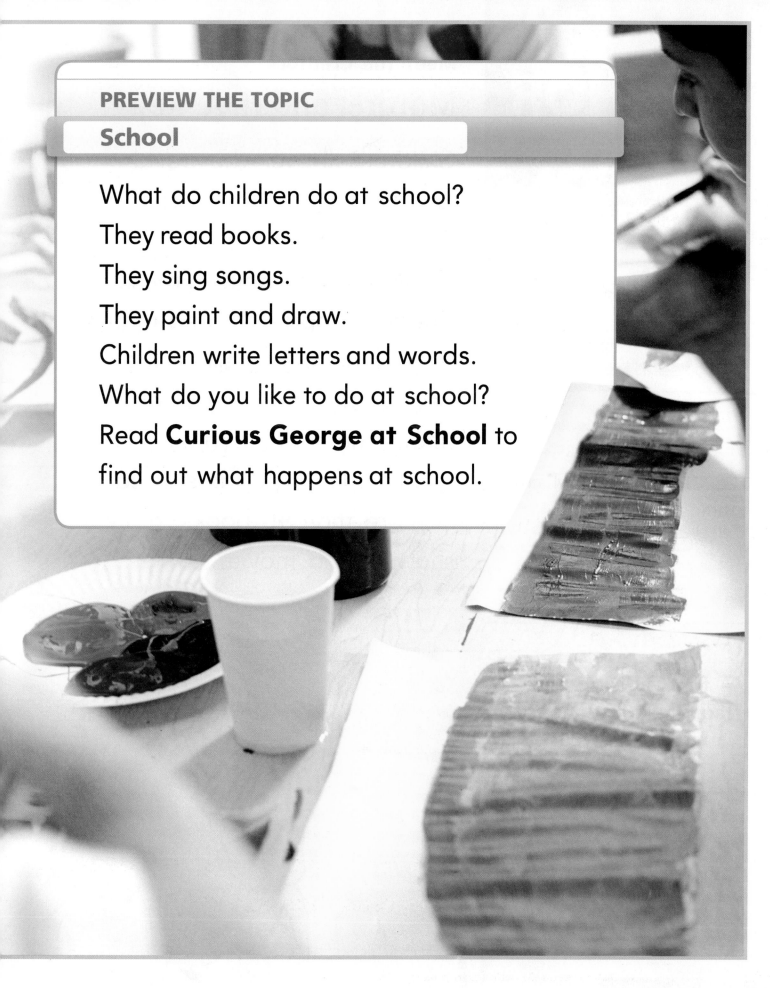

**School**

What do children do at school?

They read books.

They sing songs.

They paint and draw.

Children write letters and words.

What do you like to do at school?

Read **Curious George at School** to find out what happens at school.

# ANCHOR TEXT

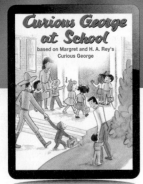

Curious George at School
based on Margret and H. A. Rey's Curious George

## ☑ TARGET SKILL

**Sequence of Events**
Tell the order in which things happen.

## ☑ GENRE

A **fantasy** is a story that could not happen in real life. As you read, look for:

▶ events that could not really happen

▶ animals that act like people

COMMON CORE  **ELACC1RL3** describe characters, settings, and major events; **ELACC1RL10** read prose and poetry

Go Digital

**Meet the Creators**

## Margret and H. A. Rey

Children all over the world love Curious George!  The Reys' books have been published in Spanish, French, Swedish, Japanese, and many other languages.  Since the Reys wrote their first book about the curious little monkey, George has starred in more than 40 books, a TV show, and a movie.

# Curious George at School

based on Margret and H. A. Rey's
Curious George

**ESSENTIAL QUESTION**

Why is going to school important?

This is George.
He can help a lot.

George can sing.
He is funny.

He can see the paints.

Mix, mix, mix a bit.
Mix, mix, mix a lot!

It is a big mess!

George ran.
What did he find?

He got a mop.
He had a big job to do.

No, no!
It is a big, BIG mess!
George is sad, sad, sad.

Kids help him do a big job.
They can help him a lot.
He is not sad!

# Dig Deeper

## How to Analyze the Text

Use these pages to learn more about Sequence of Events and Author's Word Choice. Then read **Curious George at School** again.

## Sequence of Events

In **Curious George at School**, you read about what happens to George at school. Authors write what happens in a certain order. Think about what happens **first, next,** and **last** as you read. You can use a flow chart to show the order of important events in the story.

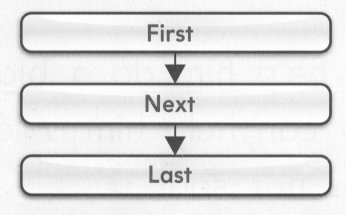

First

↓

Next

↓

Last

COMMON CORE

**ELACC1RL3** describe characters, settings, and major events

Go Digital

## Author's Word Choice

Writers choose the words they use carefully. Some words help readers picture events. Some words tell more about a character.

The story says that George is funny. What other words does the author use to describe George and the mess he makes?

funny

happy

scared

# Your Turn

## RETURN TO THE ESSENTIAL QUESTION

 **Turn and Talk**

**Why is going to school important?** Find text evidence that tells what George learns at school. Tell your partner what happens to him first, next, and last. What do you do at school that is important?

 **Classroom Conversation**

Talk about these questions with your class.

**1** How does George try to help?

**2** How do the children help George?

**3** How is George's school like your school?

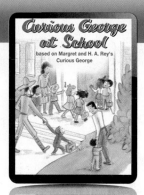

**Response** Write sentences to describe George. Tell what you think he is like. Use text evidence to give reasons why you think so.

### Writing Tip

Use the word **because** when you write reasons for your ideas.

**COMMON CORE**   **ELACC1RL2** retell stories and demonstrate understanding of the message or lesson; **ELACC1RL3** describe characters, settings, and major events; **ELACC1RL7** use illustrations and details to describe characters, setting, or events; **ELACC1W1** write opinion pieces; **ELACC1SL4** describe people, places, things, and events with details/express ideas and feelings clearly

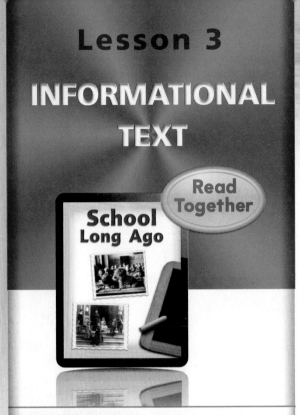

Read Together

School Long Ago

**Informational text** gives facts about a topic. This is a social studies article. Read to find out what the topic is.

A **chart** is a drawing that lists information in a clear way. What can you learn from the chart on page 88?

COMMON CORE ELACC1RI5 know and use text features to locate facts or information; ELACC1RI10 read informational texts

# School Long Ago

How did children get to school? Was going to school long ago different from going to school today? Let's find out! There were no school buses long ago. Some children had to walk far to get to school.

**What did children bring to school?**
Long ago, children did not have
backpacks. They carried their
things for school in their arms.
Children did not have a lot
of paper long ago. They
used chalk to write on small
boards called slates.

## What did children learn?

Long ago, children learned reading, writing, and math. Some teachers taught children funny songs to sing. What do children learn in school today?

| Then | Now |
|------|-----|
| | |
| | |
| | |

# Compare Texts

**Read Together**

## TEXT TO TEXT

**Compare Genres** Is the story about Curious George real or make-believe? How do you know? Tell how you know **School Long Ago** is true.

## TEXT TO SELF

**Connect to Experiences** Think of something Curious George did that you have also done. Write about it.

## TEXT TO WORLD

**Draw a Map** Draw a map of your classroom. Show where you sit. Describe your classroom to a partner.

**COMMON CORE** **ELACC1RL5** explain major differences between story books and informational books; **ELACC1W8** recall information from experiences or gather information from sources to answer a question

# Grammar

**Action Verbs** Some words tell what people and animals do. These action words are called **verbs**.

**hop**

**play**

**jog**

**hit**

Write a verb from the box to name the action in each picture. Use another sheet of paper. Then act out one of the verbs. Have a partner guess the verb.

paint    help    sip    mix

1.

2.

3.

4.

 **Grammar in Writing**

When you revise your writing, use action verbs to tell about things you do.

**ELACC1W3** write narratives; **ELACC1L1a** print upper- and lowercase letters; **ELACC1L1e** use verbs to convey sense of past, present, and future

# Narrative Writing

Read Together

my WriteSmart

Go Digital

✓ **Word Choice** Writers use exact nouns to help give readers a clear picture. What things did Leah's class do? Leah wrote about the activities. Later, she changed **things** to a noun that is exact.

## Revised Draft

books

We all read ~~things~~.
          ^

 **Writing Traits Checklist**

✓ **Word Choice** Did I use nouns that are exact?

✓ Did I use action verbs to tell what we did?

✓ Did I write letters neatly and correctly?

✓ Did I write an ending sentence?

Find nouns and verbs in Leah's final copy. Then revise your writing. Use the Checklist.

**Final Copy**

# Fun at School

We all read books.
We wrote stories.
Then we sang songs.
Today was a lot of fun!

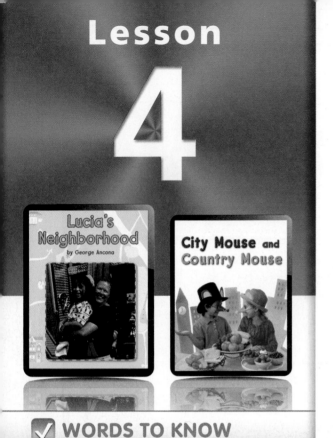

Lucia's Neighborhood
by George Ancona

City Mouse and Country Mouse

☑ **WORDS TO KNOW**
High-Frequency Words

my

here

who

all

does

me

Vocabulary Reader

Context Cards

COMMON CORE

**ELACC1RF3g** recognize and read irregularly spelled words

Go Digital

# Words to Know

▶ Read each Context Card.

▶ Tell about a picture, using the blue word.

---

**1** **my**

The dentist will check my teeth.

---

**2** **here**

The firefighters keep their trucks here.

**3** **who**

Who brings the mail to your house?

**4** **all**

The baker made all of these rolls.

**5** **does**

Does this vet take care of dogs?

**6** **me**

The zookeeper let me pet the koala.

# Read and Comprehend

Read Together

Go Digital

☑ **TARGET SKILL**

**Text and Graphic Features** Authors may use **special features** like photos, maps, and drawings to explain a topic. Labels and captions can give more information about photos. Use special features to help you get information. You can list the features and the information you learn on a chart.

| Feature | Purpose |
|---------|---------|
|         |         |
|         |         |

☑ **TARGET STRATEGY**

**Question** Ask yourself questions as you read. Look for text evidence to help you answer them.

**ELACC1RI4** ask and answer questions to determine or clarify the meaning of words and phrases; **ELACC1RI5** know and use text features to locate facts or information

## Neighborhoods

A neighborhood is where people live.

Neighbors are people who live nearby.

Neighbors help each other.

They are friendly.

How can you help your neighbors?

You will read about neighbors in **Lucia's Neighborhood.**

# ANCHOR TEXT

Lucia's
Neighborhood
by George Ancona

## ✓ TARGET SKILL

**Text and Graphic Features** Tell how the words and photos give information.

## ✓ GENRE

**Informational text** gives facts about a topic. Look for:

▶ words that tell information
▶ photographs that show details about the real world

**COMMON CORE** **ELACC1RI4** ask and answer questions to determine or clarify the meaning of words and phrases; **ELACC1RI5** know and use text features to locate facts or information; **ELACC1RI10** read informational texts

**Meet the Author and Photographer**

## George Ancona

What do you like to do for fun? George Ancona enjoys dancing, listening to salsa music, and spending time with his grandchildren. He does not like to watch TV or send e-mail. Mr. Ancona has written many books, including **Mi Música/My Music.**

35

Go Digital

# Lucia's Neighborhood

written and photographed by George Ancona

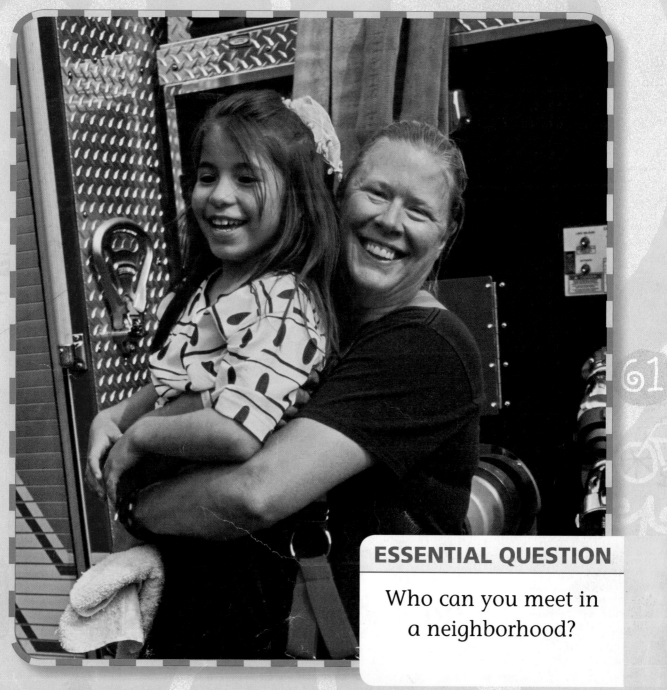

**ESSENTIAL QUESTION**

Who can you meet in a neighborhood?

Hi! I am Lucia.
Can I get a goal?

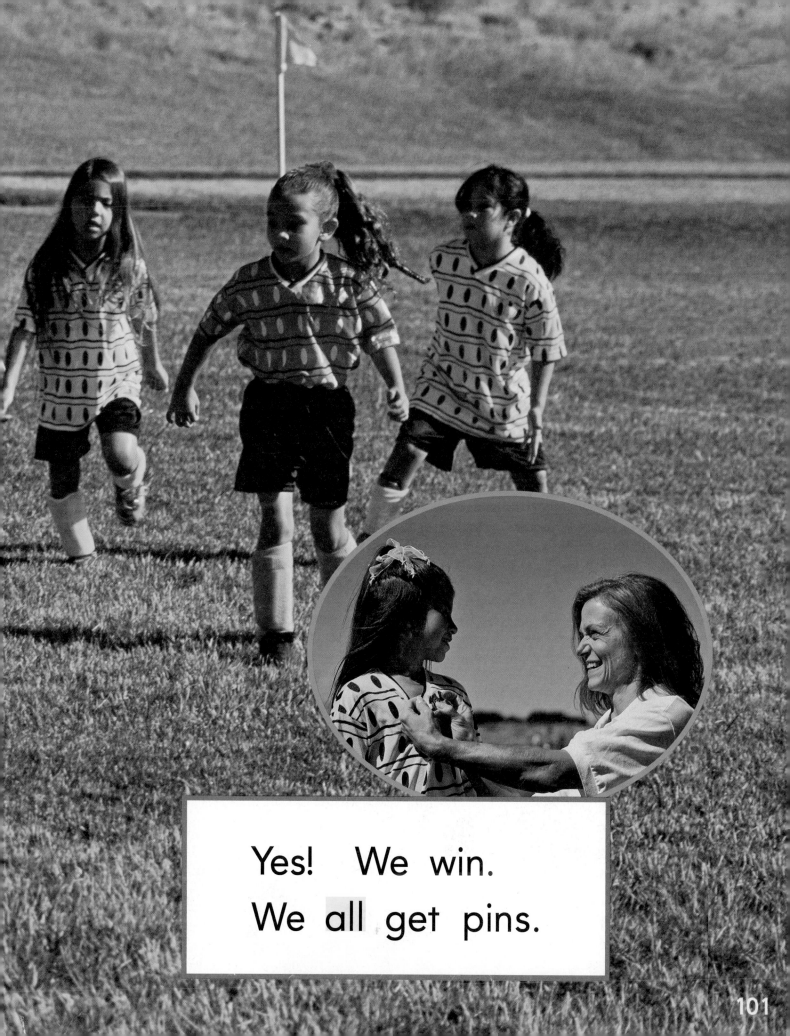

Yes! We win.
We all get pins.

**Bakery**

26

What can Mom and I do?
Look what we get here.

102

61

I can look at pets here.
It is fun.

**Plant Shop**

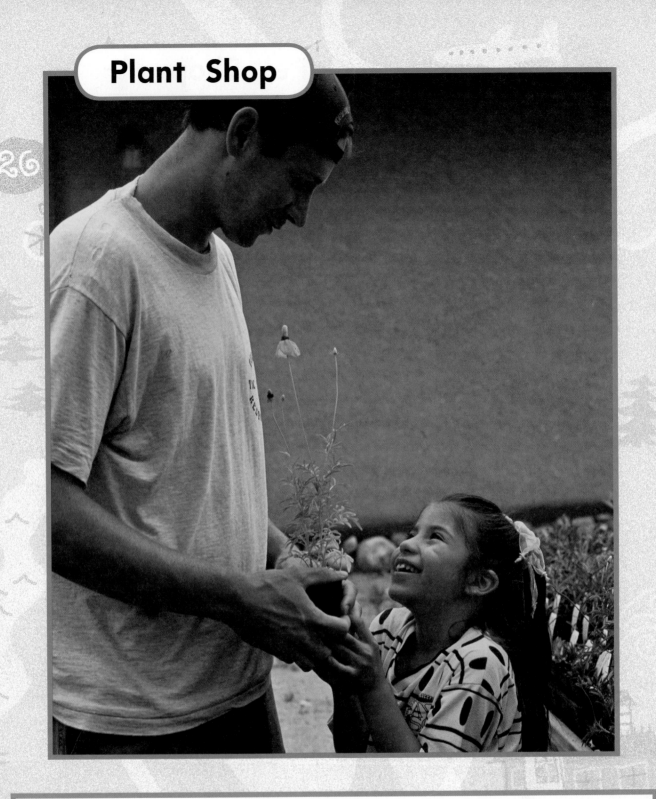

Mom let me get a plant here.
It is not big yet.

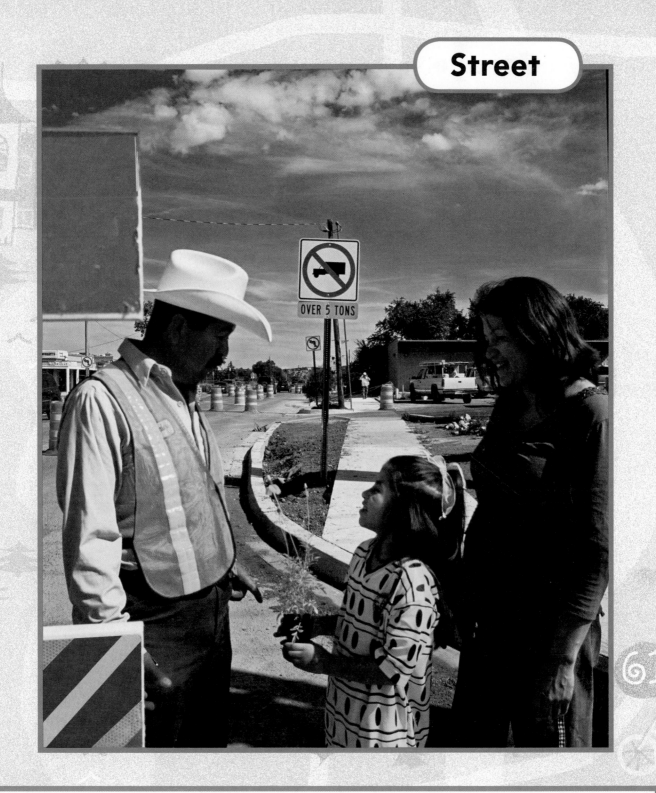

Street

Who can fix the street?
Here is the man who can fix it.

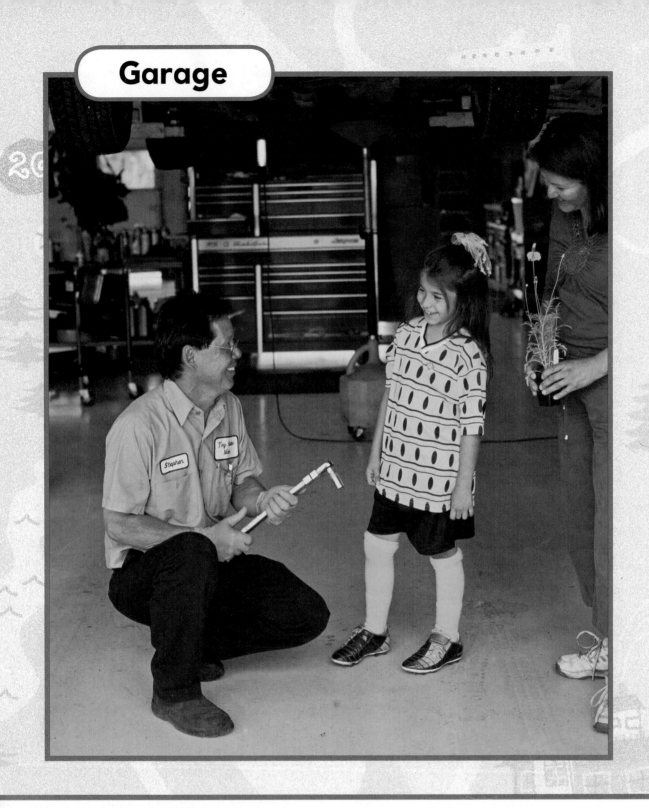

Garage

Who can fix a car?
Here is the man who can fix it.

Firehouse

61

Who has on firefighter's pants?
They are too big to fit me yet!

Library

Does the librarian help me?
Yes!
We sit and look at my book.

Is it fun to be home?
You bet it is!

# Dig Deeper

## How to Analyze the Text

Learn about Text and Graphic Features and Author's Word Choice. Then read **Lucia's Neighborhood** again.

## Text and Graphic Features

In **Lucia's Neighborhood,** the author uses special features to tell more about the neighborhood. What information do the photos show? How does each label help you find and understand the information? Use a chart to tell about the special features and the information they give.

| Feature | Purpose |
|---------|---------|
|         |         |

COMMON CORE

**ELACC1RI4** ask and answer questions to determine or clarify the meaning of words and phrases; **ELACC1RI5** know and use text features to locate facts or information

Go Digital

## Author's Word Choice

An author thinks about what words he or she will use.  Choosing certain words or phrases makes the selection fun and interesting to read.  Phrases like **on the ball** or **right as rain** are fun ways to say **perfect!**

As you read, ask yourself why the author uses the words he does.  Think about what the words really mean.

# Your Turn

 *my* **WriteSmart**

## RETURN TO THE ESSENTIAL QUESTION

 **Turn and Talk**

**Who can you meet in a neighborhood?** Find text evidence in **Lucia's Neighborhood** to answer. Then draw a picture of a person from your neighborhood. Add a label. Describe the picture to your partner.

### Classroom Conversation

Talk about these questions with your class.

1 What words can you use to tell what Lucia's neighbors are like?

2 How is Lucia's neighborhood like yours?

3 What would you like to ask Lucia about her neighborhood?

## WRITE ABOUT READING

**Response** Choose one place that Lucia visits. Write sentences that tell what the place is like. Use text evidence, such as the photo and the words on the page, to help you describe the place.

Go Digital

### Writing Tip

Begin each sentence with a capital letter. End it with a period.

COMMON CORE   **ELACC1RI7** use illustrations and details to describe key ideas; **ELACC1SL5** add drawings or visual displays to descriptions to clarify ideas, thoughts, and feelings

# FABLE

Read Together

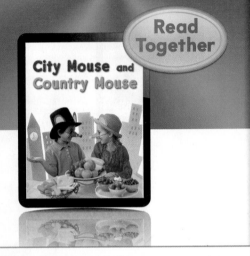

✅ **GENRE**

A **fable** is a short story in which a character learns a lesson. The characters in a fable are often animals.

✅ **TEXT FOCUS**

Fables usually end with a **story lesson**. The lesson is sometimes called a **moral**. Read this fable to find out what lesson the characters learn.

COMMON CORE **ELACC1RL2** retell stories and demonstrate understanding of the message or lesson; **ELACC1RL10** read prose and poetry

**Readers' Theater**

# City Mouse and Country Mouse

retold by Debbie O'Brien

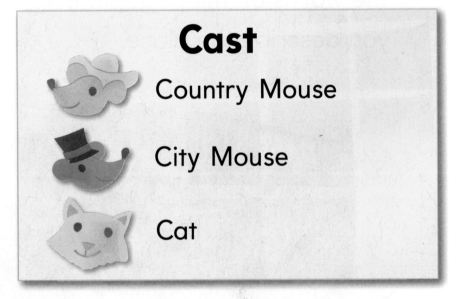

## Cast

Country Mouse

City Mouse

Cat

Once upon a time, there were two mice.

I love my country home. Come eat with me.

I like city food better.

Come with me to the city.
We will eat like kings.

 I will come.

 Here is my home.

 Look at all this yummy food!

Meow, meow. I will have mice for lunch!

 Who is that?

 It's Cat! Run and hide.

 City Mouse, my home does not have fine food, but it is safe. I'm going back to the country.

# Compare Texts

Read Together

## TEXT TO TEXT

**Compare Feelings** How do Lucia and the mice feel about their neighborhoods? How do you know?

## TEXT TO SELF

**Respond to the Story** What lesson does Country Mouse learn? Has anything like this ever happened to you? Write sentences about it.

## TEXT TO WORLD

**Discuss Neighborhoods** Who or what makes your neighborhood special? Describe to a partner. Use details.

Go Digital

 COMMON CORE **ELACC1RL2** retell stories and demonstrate understanding of the message or lesson; **ELACC1RL9** compare and contrast adventures and experiences of characters; **ELACC1RI9** identify similarities in and differences between texts on the same topic; **ELACC1W8** recall information from experiences or gather information from sources to answer a question; **ELACC1SL4** describe people, places, things, and events with details/express ideas and feelings clearly

# Grammar

**Adjectives** Some words describe people, animals, places, or things. These describing words are called **adjectives**. Adjectives can describe by telling size or shape.

## Adjectives for Size

tall

long

short

tiny

## Adjectives for Shape

round

oval

curved

thin

flat

**Try This!**

Think of an adjective for size or shape to describe each picture. Write the word on another sheet of paper. Use the adjective in a sentence.

1.

2.

3.

4.

5.

 **Grammar in Writing**

When you revise your class story, look for places to add adjectives to tell what things look like.

**ELACC1W3** write narratives; **ELACC1W5** focus on a topic, respond to questions/suggestions from peers, and add details to strengthen writing; **ELACC1L1b** use common, proper, and possessive nouns; **ELACC1L1f** use frequently occurring adjectives

**Reading-Writing Workshop: Revise**

# Narrative Writing

✅ **Word Choice** When you write a **class story**, choose interesting words that are just right!

Ms. Soto's class wrote about their town. Later, they changed **big** to a clearer word.

## Revised Draft

Our town has a big parade.

tall
Funny clowns wear ~~big~~ hats.
          ^

## Revising Checklist

✅ Does our story have interesting details?

✅ Did we use nouns that are exact?

✅ Did we use adjectives to tell about size or shape?

✅ Did we write a sentence to end the story?

Read our class story. Find adjectives. Find words that tell order. Now help revise your class story. Use the Checklist.

**Final Copy**

# Our Town Parade

Our town has a big parade.
Funny clowns wear tall hats.
A fire truck blasts its horn.
Horses prance down wide streets.
At the end, a loud band marches by.

☑ **WORDS TO KNOW**
High-Frequency Words

**many**
**friend**
**full**
**pull**
**hold**
**good**

Vocabulary Reader

Context Cards

**ELACC1RF3g** recognize and read irregularly spelled words

Go Digital

# Words to Know

**Read Together**

▶ **Read each Context Card.**

▶ **Use a blue word to tell about something you did.**

**1** **many**

There are many cars on the street.

**2** **friend**

She likes to ride the bus with her friend.

### 3 full

This train is always full of people.

### 4 pull

He can pull his pet in the wagon.

### 5 hold

She can hold her phone in her hand.

### 6 good

The ferry is a good way to see the city.

# Read and Comprehend

Read Together

Go Digital

☑ **TARGET SKILL**

**Story Structure** A story has different parts. The **characters** are the people and animals in a story. The **setting** is when and where it takes place. The **plot** is the story events. It is the problem the characters have and how they solve it. You can use a story map to tell who is in a story, where they are, and what they do.

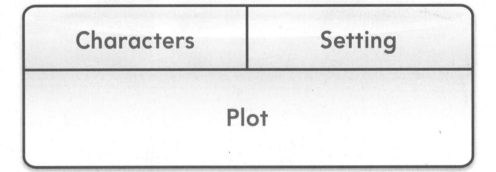

| Characters | Setting |
|---|---|
| Plot | |

☑ **TARGET STRATEGY**

**Analyze/Evaluate** Tell what you think of the story. Give text evidence to tell why.

## At the Zoo

What can you see at the zoo?

There are many animals, like bears!

You can watch the monkeys swing.

You can hear the lions roar.

Which animal is your favorite?

You will read about a trip to the zoo in **Gus Takes the Train.**

# ANCHOR TEXT

Gus Takes the Train
...by Russell Benfanti

## ✓ TARGET SKILL

**Story Structure** Tell about the setting, characters, and events in a story.

## ✓ GENRE

A **fantasy** is a story that could not happen in real life. As you read, look for:

▶ events that could not really happen

▶ animal characters who act like people

COMMON CORE **ELACC1RL3** describe characters, settings, and major events; **ELACC1RL7** use illustrations and details to describe characters, setting, or events; **ELACC1RL10** read prose and poetry

🖥 Go Digital

**Meet the Author and Illustrator**

## Russell Benfanti

If you like Russell Benfanti's colorful artwork, then visit a toy store. There you will find board games, toy packages, and computer games that Mr. Benfanti designed. "I love what I do!" he says.

# Gus Takes the Train

written and illustrated by Russell Benfanti

**ESSENTIAL QUESTION**

What happens on the train?

Gus has to run to get the train.
He has a big bag to pull.

Run, Gus, run!

Gus cannot pull up his bag.
The conductor can help him.

The train is full.
Gus can see many kids.

Gus sat.

His big bag can go up here.

Gus met a friend!
Peg and Gus sing and play.

Peg can hold the cups for Gus.
They are too full!

Peg and Gus have a sip.
It is good!

Gus can see a lot.
A funny bug is on the window!

We are here!
Gus had fun on the train.

# Dig Deeper

Read Together

## How to Analyze the Text

Use these pages to learn more about
Story Structure and Fantasy. Then read
**Gus Takes the Train** again.

## Story Structure

**Gus Takes the Train** has **characters,
settings,** and a **plot**. All of these work
together to tell the story. Who are the
characters? Where are they in different
parts of the story? Write text evidence on
a story map to tell who is in the story,
where they are, and what they do.

| Characters | Settings |
|------------|----------|
| Plot ||

ELACC1RL3 describe characters, settings, and major events; **ELACC1RL7** use illustrations and details to describe characters, setting, or events

COMMON CORE

Go Digital

## Genre: Fantasy

This story is a **fantasy**. That means it is make-believe and could not happen in real life. In the story, Gus sings. Can cats sing a song in real life?

Look again at the pictures in the story. Do they look like real life? What text evidence tells you that this story is a fantasy?

# Your Turn

 my WriteSmart

## RETURN TO THE ESSENTIAL QUESTION

 Turn and Talk

**What happens on the train?** Tell what Gus does first, next, and last. Then draw a picture of something Gus will see at the zoo. Describe it. Show your picture as you talk to help explain your ideas.

 **Classroom Conversation**

Talk about these questions with your class.

1 Why does Gus take the train?

2 How does Peg help Gus?

3 Think about the end of the story. What will Gus do next?

# WRITE ABOUT READING

**Response** Write the story the way Peg would tell it. Write sentences to tell what happens at the beginning, middle, and end of the story.

## Writing Tip

Add words like **first, next,** and **last** to tell when things happen.

# INFORMATIONAL TEXT

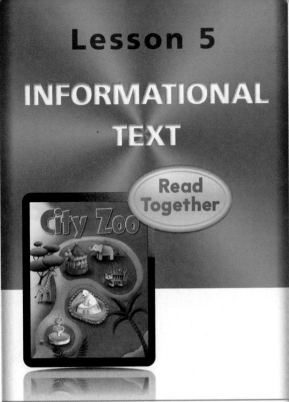

Read Together

✓ **GENRE**

**Informational text** gives facts about a topic. It can be from a magazine, brochure, or website. What is the topic of this selection?

✓ **TEXT FOCUS**

A **map** is a drawing of a place. It can help you to get somewhere. A **key** shows what pictures on the map mean. What does each picture in the key on page 143 mean?

COMMON CORE · **ELACC1RI5** know and use text features to locate facts or information; **ELACC1RI10** read informational texts

# City Zoo

Welcome to the City Zoo! The zoo is full of many interesting animals. See if you can find all the animals on the map.

**Key**

tiger

elephant

polar bear

giraffe

We hope you have a good time at the zoo.

- Come with your family and a friend.

- Hold on to your ticket.

- Have some snacks.

- Pull a wagon.

- Take pictures.

# Compare Texts

Read Together

## TEXT TO TEXT

**Compare Selections** Think about both selections. Tell which is make-believe and which is true. Tell how you know.

## TEXT TO SELF

**Write a Description** Write to tell your classmates about a time you went on a trip. Tell them what you saw and did.

## TEXT TO WORLD

**Connect to Social Studies** Imagine that you are traveling to study animals. Where would you go? Find that place on a map or globe. Describe your trip. Use details.

Go Digital

COMMON CORE **ELACC1RL5** explain major differences between story books and informational books; **ELACC1W8** recall information from experiences or gather information from sources to answer a question; **ELACC1SL4** describe people, places, things, and events with details/express ideas and feelings clearly

# Grammar

**Adjectives** Some **adjectives** describe people, animals, places, or things by telling their color or how many.

**Adjectives for Color**

purple    red    green

blue    orange    black

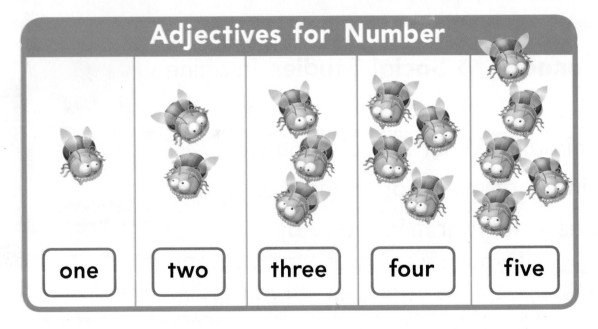

**Adjectives for Number**

one    two    three    four    five

Write one number adjective and one color adjective to describe each item. Talk with your partner about how adjectives help tell what things are like.

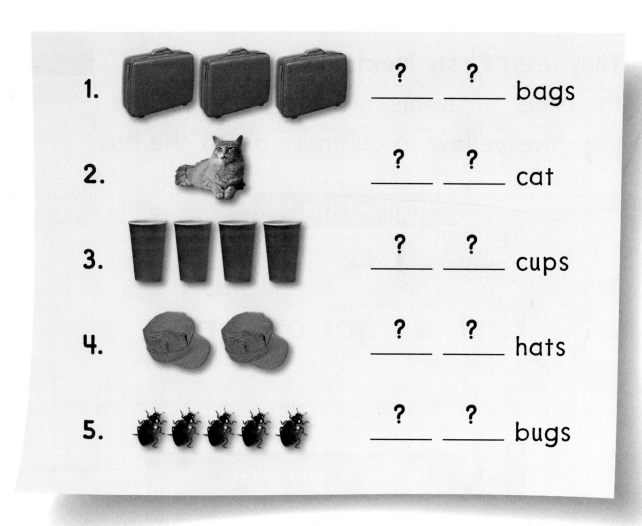

1. ___?___ ___?___ bags

2. ___?___ ___?___ cat

3. ___?___ ___?___ cups

4. ___?___ ___?___ hats

5. ___?___ ___?___ bugs

##  Grammar in Writing

When you revise your writing, look for places where you can add adjectives to tell what things are like.

ELACC1W3 write narratives; ELACC1W5 focus on a topic, respond to questions/suggestions from peers, and add details to strengthen writing;
ELACC1L1f use frequently occurring adjectives

**Reading-Writing Workshop: Revise**

# Narrative Writing

Read Together

☑ **Ideas** When you write a **class story,** use adjectives to describe things clearly.

Mr. Tam's class wrote about a bus trip. They used **First, Next,** and **Last** to tell the order of events.  Then they added the adjective **yellow** to tell more about the bus.

---

**Revised Draft**

First, we got on a ∧ bus.
yellow

---

**Revising Checklist**

☑ Are the story events in the correct order?

☑ Did we use words like **First, Next,** and **Last** to show the order?

☑ Could we tell more by adding adjectives?

Read our class story. Find adjectives. Find words that tell order. Now help revise your class story. Use the Checklist.

**Final Copy**

# A City Bus Ride

Our class took a bus trip.

First, we got on a yellow bus.

Next, we sang two songs.

Last, we saw tall buildings and long trains.

We had fun on our class trip.

Read each story. As you read, stop and answer each question. Use text evidence.

# A Pet for Tim

My dad said, "Tim, you can get a pet."

My friends have pets I like.

Dan has Mac the dog.

Mac likes to run and play.

A dog is a fun pet.

---

❶  Why does Tim think a dog is a good pet?

---

**ELACC1RL1** ask and answer questions about key details; **ELACC1RL2** retell stories and demonstrate understanding of the message or lesson; **ELACC1RL3** describe characters, settings, and major events; **ELACC1RL10** read prose and poetry

Jed has Bev the bird.

It can sing and speak.

It says funny things.

Bev stays in.

Mel has Dot the cat.

All she does is stay in and nap!

I want a pet that can go out.

❷ Retell the story. Which pet do you think
Tim will get? Why?

# Fun at the Zoo

Pam and Mom go to the zoo.

First, they go to see the cubs.

The cubs hop in the mud.

They make a big mess!

Next, they see the big cats.

The big cats nap in the sun.

---

**❸** Describe what Pam and Mom see **first** and **next.**

---

Last, Pam and Mom go to see the funny seals.

The man chooses Pam to help him.

Pam helps him with the fish.

Pam and Mom have fun at the zoo!

---

**❹** What is the main idea of this story? What details help you know?

---

# Words to Know

G1

## Unit 1   High-Frequency Words

**❶ What Is a Pal?**
play
be
and
help
with
you

**❷ The Storm**
he
look
have
for
too
what

**❸ Curious George at School**
sing
do
they
find
no
funny

**❹ Lucia's Neighborhood**
my
here
who
all
does
me

**❺ Gus Takes the Train**
many
friend
full
pull
hold
good

# B

**bed**

A **bed** is a kind of furniture for sleeping.
I sleep in my **bed**.

**book**

A **book** is a group of pages with words on them.
**Frog and Toad** is my favorite **book**.

# C

**car**

A **car** is a machine with
four wheels. We go in a
**car** to visit my grandparents.

**come**

To **come** means to move toward something.
Maria called the puppy to **come** to her.

## conductor

The **conductor** is the person in charge of a train.
The train **conductor** watched the tracks closely.

## curious

To be **curious** is to want to learn.  Alan was **curious**
about dinosaurs.

# F

## firefighter's

A **firefighter** is someone
who puts out fires.  A
**firefighter's** job can
be dangerous.

## fun

To have **fun** is to have a
good time.  The children
had **fun** playing tag.

# G

**George**
**George** is a boy's name. My son's name is **George**.

**goal**
A **goal** is a score in a game. Anita kicked the ball and made a **goal**.

# H

**hi**
The word **hi** means hello. I say **hi** when I see someone I know.

**home**
A **home** is a place where people or animals live. There are six people living in my **home**.

# J

**job**
A **job** is work for people to do. Uncle Ned has a **job** in a store.

# K

## kids

**Kid** is another word for child.
My uncle tells funny stories about
when he and my dad were **kids**.

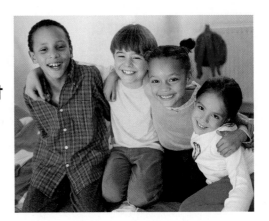

# L

## librarian

A **librarian** works in a place where many books are kept.
The **librarian** helped me find the book I was looking for.

## Lucia

**Lucia** is a girl's name.  My sister's name is **Lucia**.

# M

## mess

A **mess** is something that is not neat.  My sister's room
is a **mess!**

# N

**neighborhood**

A **neighborhood** is a part of a city or town.
Jim walks to the store in his **neighborhood**.

# P

**paints**

**Paints** are liquids with colors in them.
Dip the big brushes into the **paints**.

**pal**

A **pal** is a friend. Benny is
my best **pal**.

**pants**

People wear **pants** over their legs.
Lucy's **pants** have two big pockets.

**pet**

A **pet** is an animal who lives with you.
My cat Sam is the best **pet** ever!

### plant

A **plant** is anything alive that is not a person or an animal. We have a **plant** with big green leaves in our kitchen.

### Pop

**Pop** is one name for a grandfather. I call my mother's father **Pop**.

# S

### school

A **school** is a place where students learn from teachers. I learn to read at **school**.

### storm

A **storm** is strong wind, rain, or snow. Lots of rain fell during the **storm**.

### street

A **street** is a road in a city or a town. We live on a very busy **street**.

# T

**takes**

The word **takes** can mean to travel by.
Mia **takes** the bus to school.

**this**

**This** means something that is near you.
**This** is the book I'm taking home.

**train**

A **train** is a group of railroad
cars.  This summer my family
is going on a **train** ride.

# W

**wet**

**Wet** means covered with liquid.  Juan got
**wet** when he went out in the rain.

**what**

The word **what** is used to ask questions.
**What** did you eat for breakfast?

**window**

A **window** is an open place
in a wall.  Sasha opened
the **window.**

# Acknowledgments

*Curious George at School*, text by Houghton Mifflin Harcourt Publishing, illustrated by Margret and H.A. Rey. Copyright ©2011 by Houghton Mifflin Harcourt Publishing Company. All rights reserved. The character Curious George® including without limitation the character's name and the character's likeness are registered trademarks of Houghton Mifflin Harcourt Publishing Company. Curious George logo is a trademark of Houghton Mifflin Harcourt Publishing Company.

"Damon & Blue" from *My Man Blue* by Nikki Grimes. Copyright ©1999 by Nikki Grimes. Reprinted by permission of Dial Books for Young Readers, a division of Penguin Young Readers Group, a member of Penguin Group (USA) Inc., 345 Hudson Street, New York, NY 10014 and Curtis Brown, Ltd.

"Jambo" from *Nightfeathers* by Sundaira Morninghouse. Copyright ©1989 by Sundaira Morninghouse. Reprinted by permission of Open Hand Publishing, LLC (www.openhand.com).

"Wait for Me" by Sarah Wilson from *June Is a Tune That Jumps on a Stair*. Copyright ©1992 by Sarah Wilson. Reprinted by permission of the author.

# Credits

**Placement Key:**
(r) right, (l) left, (c) center, (t) top, (b) bottom, (bg) background

**Photo Credits**
**3** (cl) © Rommel/Masterfile; **3** (bl) ©Colin Hogan/Alamy; **4** (bl) © Douglas Keister/Corbis; **5** (bl) ©Underwood Archives; **5** (bl) ullstein bild / The Granger Collection; **5** (bl) Comstock/Fotosearch; **6** (bl) ©George Ancona; **6** (br) ©George Ancona; **6** (tl) ©George Ancona; **10** © Ariel Skelley/CORBIS; **10** (b) © Ariel Skelley/CORBIS; **10** (tl) © Rommel/Masterfile; **10** (tc) ©Colin Hogan/Alamy; **11** (tl) ©Bob Krist/Corbis; **11** (tr) Ariel Skelley/CORBIS; **11** (br) ©Paul Austring Photography/First Light/Getty Images; **11** (bl) ©Dirk Anschutz/Stone/Getty Images; **13** ©Brand X Pictures/Getty Images; **14** © Rommel/Masterfile; **15** (t) © Rommel/Masterfile; **26** © Rommel/Masterfile; **27** © Rommel/Masterfile; **28** Ryan McVey/Photodisc/Getty Images; **29** © Rommel/Masterfile; **30** © Heide Benser/Corbis; **30** ©Colin Hogan/Alamy; **32** ©Colin Hogan/Alamy; **32** ©Colin Hogan/Alamy; **33** (tl) © Rommel/Masterfile; **33** ©Colin Hogan/Alamy; **34** (cl) © Photodisc / Alamy; **34** (bl) ©Juniors Bildarchiv/Alamy; **35** (tl) © Julian Winslow/Corbis; **35** (bl) ©Rachel Watson/Stone/Getty Images; **35** (cr) © Look Photography/Beateworks/Corbis; **35** (bl) © Patrick Bennett/CORBIS; **35** Corbis; **38** (br) © Nancy G Fire Photography, Nancy Greifenhagen/Alamy Images; **38** (t) ©Amy Etra/PhotoEdit; **38** (tc) © Douglas Keister/Corbis; **39** (cr) ©Jupiter Images/Comstock Images/Alamy; **39** (tr) ©Thomas Barwick/Riser/Getty Images; **39** (tl) ©Sascha Pflaeging/Riser/Getty Images; **39** (cl) ©Richard Hutchings/PhotoEdit; **40** Corbis; **55** Ryan McGinnis/Flickr/Getty Images; **57** Bananastock/Jupiterimages/Getty Images; **58** (c) © Douglas Keister/Corbis; **58** © Douglas Keister/Corbis; **60** (tr) ©comstock/Getty Images; **60** (c) ©Photodisc/Don Farrall, Lightworks Studio/Getty Images; **60** (cr) © Authors Image / Alamy; **60** (tl) © David Young-Wolff / PhotoEdit; **60** (bl) © matthiasengelien.com/Alamy; **61** ©Kenneth Langford/Corbis; **61** (b) ©GlowImages/Alamy; **61** © Douglas Keister/Corbis; **66** (c) © Michael Newman / PhotoEdit; **66** (tc) ©Underwood Archives; **66** (tc) ullstein

bild / The Granger Collection; **66** (tc) Comstock/ Fotosearch; **67** (tl) ©Stuart Pearce/Age FotoStock; **67** (br) © David Young-Wolff / PhotoEdit; **67** (tr) Comstock/Getty Images; **68** JUPITERIMAGES/ BananaStock / Alamy; **85** Digital Vision/Getty Images; **86** (b) ©Underwood Archives; **86** (tl) ©Underwood Archives; **86** (tl) ullstein bild / The Granger Collection; **86** (tl) Comstock/Fotosearch; **87** (tc) ullstein bild / The Granger Collection; **87** (tl) Comstock/Fotosearch; **88** (tr) ©Corbis; **88** (r) Comstock/Fotosearch; **88** (cr) Brand X Pictures/ fotosearch.com; **88** (bl) © JUPITERIMAGES/ PHOTOS.COM / Alamy; **88** (br) PhotoDisc/ Getty Images; **88** (cl) ©Underwood Archives; **89** (cr) ©OJO Images/Getty Images; **89** (tl) ©Underwood Archives; **89** (tl) ullstein bild / The Granger Collection; **89** (tl) Comstock/ Fotosearch; **94** (tc) © Kelly Redinger/Design Pics/Corbis; **94** (b) ©Richard Hamilton Smith/ Corbis; **94** (tl) ©George Ancona; **95** (cr) LOOK Die Bildagentur der Fotografen GmbH/Alamy; **95** (tl) © Michael Macor/San Francisco Chronicle/ Corbis; **95** (bl) © Corbis; **95** (tr) ©Andersen Ross/ Digital Vision/Getty Images; **96** (tl) ©George Ancona; **97** (bg) Jupiterimages/Getty Images; **98** (cr) ©George Ancona; **98** (tl) ©George Ancona; **99** (b) ©George Ancona; **100** ©George Ancona; **101** ©George Ancona; **102** ©George Ancona; **103** ©George Ancona; **104** ©George Ancona; **105** ©George Ancona; **106** ©George Ancona; **107** ©George Ancona; **108** ©George Ancona; **109** ©George Ancona; **110** (tl) ©George Ancona; **111** (b) © David Buffington\Getty Images; **112** (br) C Squared Studios/Photodisc/Getty Images; **113** (tr) ©George Ancona; **117** (tc) ©George Ancona; **119** (bl) ©Chad Ehlers/Photographer's Choice/Getty Images; **119** (cl) BrandXpictures/ Burke/Triolo; **119** (tr) ©PhotoDisc/Getty Images; **119** (tl) ©Image Idea/Fotosearch; **122** (bc) © Michael Newman / PhotoEdit; **122** (c) ©Mitchell Funk/Photographer's Choice/Getty Images; **123** (cl) ©Veer; **123** (tl) © Digital Vision Ltd. / SuperStock; **123** (tr) © Michael Newman / PhotoEdit; **123** (br) ©Masterfile; **124** ATTILA KISBENEDEK/AFP/Getty Images; **139** ©Stockbyte/Alamy Images; **141** (c) Fotosonline / Alamy; **145** (br) Getty Images/Stockdisc; **145** (tr) © Ed Bohon/CORBIS; **147** (b) ©Photos. com/JupiterImages; **147** (b) ©Photodisc/Getty Images; **147** (t) ©Skip Nail/Digital Vision/Getty Images; **149** (b) ©Thomas Northcut/Getty

Images; **G2** © Adisa/Shutterstock; **G3** ©Andersen Ross/Photodisc/Getty Images; **G4** Ryan McVay/ Photodisc/Getty Images; **G5** © Getty Images; **G6** © Comstock, Inc./JupiterImages; **G7** C Squared Studios/Photodisc/Getty Images; **G8** ©PhotoDisc/ Getty Images; **G9** © Comstock, Inc./JupiterImages

## Illustrations

**Cover** John Shroades; **4** Raúl Colón; **30–32** Rick Powell; **36–37** Ken Bowser; **42–53** Raúl Colón; **62** Bernard Adnet; **54–65** Ken Bowser; **98–109** (art background) Ken Bowser; **115–116** (props) Pamela Thompson; **114–116** Bob Barner; **118** Bernard Adnet; **126–137** Russell Benfanti; **142– 144** Claudine Gevry.


All other photos: Houghton Mifflin Harcourt Photo Libraries and Photographers.